MW01226518

Tim Bless you
God Bless you
& thank you
for all that you do.

Podie Lorrie

Poetic Prayers

for
Uniformed Professionals

(Armed Forces, Police, Peace Officers, Firefighters, Customs, Security and Correctional Officers, Etc.)

Dr. Lorne K. Freake, Ph.D. (Padré)

authorHOUSE®

AuthorHouse™
1663 Liberty Drive
Bloomington, IN 47403
www.authorhouse.com
Phone: 1-800-839-8640

© 2012 by Dr. Lorne K. Freake, Ph.D. (Padré). All rights reserved.

No part of this book may be reproduced, stored in a retrieval system, or transmitted by any means without the written permission of the author.

Published by AuthorHouse   05/24/2012

ISBN: 978-1-4685-9613-7 (sc)
ISBN: 978-1-4685-9612-0 (hc)
ISBN: 978-1-4685-9611-3 (e)

Library of Congress Control Number: 2012907776

Any people depicted in stock imagery provided by Thinkstock are models, and such images are being used for illustrative purposes only.
Certain stock imagery © Thinkstock.

This book is printed on acid-free paper.

Because of the dynamic nature of the Internet, any web addresses or links contained in this book may have changed since publication and may no longer be valid. The views expressed in this work are solely those of the author and do not necessarily reflect the views of the publisher, and the publisher hereby disclaims any responsibility for them.

Scriptures quoted in this book are taken from the Good News Translation (GNT) of the Holy Bible, copyright @ 1994 by the Canadian Bible Society and New Revised Standard Version (NRSV) of the Holy Bible, Division of Christian Education of the National Council of Churches of Christ of the USA. New York, New York, copyright @ 1989, used by permission.

While the author has been a member of various professional chaplaincy associations such as: the Federation of Fire Chaplains (FFC), The Canadian Association of Police Chaplains (CAPC) and the International Police Chaplains Association (IPCA) and others, the material and values expressed in this book do not necessarily reflect the values of those professional associations. Furthermore, the book does not reflect necessarily the values of the publishing company: AuthorHouse, Inc.

Contents

Preface

We will forever be scarred by the events of 9-11. Since September 11th, 2001 our world has been changed. Most of us even now, years later can easily remember where we were when the planes hit the twin towers in New York City on 9-11.

For most of the police officers, firefighters, ambulance personnel, and other uniformed professionals out there, they started their shifts at work as they did the day before . . . yet on that day their lives would be forever changed. Unfortunately more than 100 of those precious professionals in uniform did not return home on that horrible day but lost their lives on duty while trying to help their fellow citizens.

Every year since we have taken the time in the month of September to mourn their loss and yet to celebrate their lives and the cause of freedom represented by these loses. We will do it again in September of this year and next year and the next . . .

In my own parish like many others across the country on both sides of the Canada/USA border, we have taken time to remember them year after year since, in an annual solemn September service.

We have proudly displayed the Flag and we sang our National Anthem. We displayed on the communion table at the front of the church a pair of white gloves, a police officer's and firefighter's dress uniform hats. We invited the local uniformed professionals to the service and asked them to participate in creative ways. Some were asked to help in the reading the scriptures or leading in the responsive readings. Others played a special on a musical instrument. Still others were asked to bring public greetings on behalf of the Emergency Services Department which they represented.

It was through these yearly encounters that I saw and felt the great need to become involved as an emergency services chaplain. I attempted to reach out to these uniformed men and women through pastoral care and moral support. Yes, I recognize that many of them have their own faith groups, their own religion or denomination as it were, yet I noted how difficult it was at times for them, amidst night shifts and out of town training, etc. to be able to connect to their particular faith groups. For some, it was almost impossible.

To make a long story shorter, as a parish minister, I then became a volunteer Police Chaplain, having been sworn officially into that role. I began shortly afterwards as a chaplain for the local Fire Department (GFFD) here in Grand Falls, in New Brunswick.

These are great opportunities for ministry. It includes the offering of insight, guidance, counselling, pastoral care and moral support on occasion, the 'ministry of pastoral presence'. I wear the uniform at special events. I have a pager that allows me to respond 24/7 to the calls. When I'm available, I am able to do 'Ride-Alongs', depending on the circumstances. A 'Ride-Along' is an excellent opportunity to build camaraderie in the good times so pastoral contact is then made easier in the more difficult times.

As volunteer chaplains, we are sometimes available for prayer and counselling for our uniformed professionals, but we're not available all the time. Let's say, "We're not 'pastorally present' all the time due to our own work schedules, family responsibilities, travel, etc." Hence, it is with this reality that I came to realize the necessity to write a series of handbooks for our uniformed professionals so that they could easily access some measure of pastoral care and tangible moral support on their own. From that reflection, comes a six volume set of pastoral helps for men and women in uniform. What you are holding in your hand at present is Volume One. I have entitled it "Poetic Prayers For Uniformed Professionals . . ."

In an genuine effort to avoid dull prayers, full of meaningless words that are seen as 'boring' at best, I have intentionally written them with some rhythm so that they are not only easy to meditate on if desired, but easy to pray aloud if preferred.

As beauty is in the 'eyes of the beholder', so is poetry in the 'ears of the hearer'. Hence, as the author (poet) of these poetic prayers, I note that the poems flow very well because of where I place the emphasis. Depending on where it is placed by you the reader, will evidently determine how well it flows.

In this volume are 18 prayers. These are not prayers for special occasions, although that is an idea for a future volume in this series. These are prayers for eighteen different situations that might arise in the life of any uniformed professional. These prayers are specifically for those who work in emergency services or at least have the possibility of finding themselves having to face an emergency or two on the daily job. In the Table of Contents is listed a series of prayers that serves to address almost every possible situation in the life of a uniformed professional. Please look out for Volume II in the series which is entitled "Helpful Homilies for Uniformed Professionals" and then Volume III entitled "Reflective Readings for Uniformed Professionals". Then Volume IV, etc. Stay tuned. Enjoy.

Foreword

BY
DR. MARY SPEED

Dr. Freake's prose is touching and fitting for each of the topics that he has chosen for this text. He has found a way to give voice to insiders and those outside the emergency responder professions.

One recognizes in *Prayers for Uniformed Professionals* that all are somehow connected to the services rendered. Grief is no respecter of persons.

This text is a wonderful addition to the volumes of works that Dr. Freake is contributing to.

We are fortunate that Dr. Freake is so willing to share his voice giving all of us words of solace.

You will be glad that you have this book on your shelf. In the night, when you need an immediate word of help, *Prayers for Uniformed Professionals* will be the book to reach for in that time of need.

Acknowledgements

I want to express thankfulness to two area churches who saw this project as an excellent means of ministering to our nation's uniformed professionals: *Sisson Ridge United Baptist Church* in Sisson Ridge, New Brunswick and *Family Worship Center* in Grand Falls, New Brunswick, Canada.

I also want to thank and honour the families of two 'Uniformed Professionals'. First of all for:

MR. RALPH ELLIOT
October 26, 1920-December 21, 2001

who was a member of the Royal Artillery 59th Newfoundland  Regiment, 23rd Battery, as a Gunner. He served overseas July 29, 1940 to July 30, 1945 and was honourably discharged September 29, 1945. He served in England, France, Belgium, the Netherlands and Germany. He received several medals for his service. He was awarded the Dutch Medal of Honour after his death. He is survived by wife Selena, son Guy, daughters Sylvia, Sophie, Glenda, Naida and Mary and 11 grandchildren. His favourite Bible verse was Isaiah 40:31.

Secondly, I also want to thank and honour the family of a 'Uniformed Professional' by the name of

PAUL JOSEPH GREEN
(December 13th, 1950 - October 9th, 2008)

who served with the Perth-Andover Fire Department in Perth-Andover, New Brunswick. Mr. Green was a dedicated member of the Perth-Andover Fire Dept from 1987 to 2008. He served in roles of Training Officer, Captain and Assistant Chief. He is survived by his lovely wife, Barbara and two sons, who are also uniformed professionals. They are: Jason who is a firefighter in Perth-Andover, NB and Joel in the Canadian Forces at Petawawa, Ontario. There are also three grandchildren: Anson and Ainsley of Perth-Andover, NB and Sutherland (Sully) of Petawawa, Ontario. Thank you Paul, God bless you and yours.

Dedication

This little book is written in dedication to the many brave men and women (uniformed professionals) who put their lives in harms way, day after day. This book is written for you, in order for you to have another tool in your tool kit for your daily work and for private life. God bless you all and thanks for your tireless efforts!

Prologue

When you pass through the waters, I will be with you; and through the rivers, they shall not overwhelm you; when you walk through fire you shall not be burned, and the flame shall not consume you. For I am the Lord your God . . . Isaiah 43:2-3a (**NRSV**)

Introduction

Life is hard. It is at times the school of hard knocks! Yet there is a presence that goes with us. This presence is real and divine. It manifests itself in the abstract, the invisible, the silence and yet in the tangible, the visible and in words.

The Spirit of God is present, simply because He is there. The Spirit is also present because of the presence of his servants (chaplains), the 'pastorally present' men and women of the cloth, who are there to offer spiritual guidance, pastoral care and moral support.

These are the people who uniform professionals have access to for prayer, guidance and someone who will lend a listening ear.

As a police and fire department chaplain, let me encourage you as a uniformed professional to contact your chaplain whether you are a religious person or not. The use of chaplaincy service does not assume any religious affiliation or faith, nor does it assume the lack thereof.

This book is not intended to replace your valuable chaplaincy services. It is neither intended to replace the pastoral care you might receive in your own faith community. It is simply another tool in your tool kit of life to help you along the way. This book has poetic prayers that I suspect you will pray more than once. The prayers are listed likely in chronological order from early in your career up to retirement including many possible crisis along the way.

The Gospels record that Christ Himself at times, had to go away from the hustle and bustle of life in order to pray. Prayer gets us closer to God. It helps charge our spiritual batteries. It revives us, enables us to rest, to relieve and ultimately to refocus. If Christ Himself had to take time from his busy schedule for prayer, as a uniformed professional, you may need to do likewise.

Prayer by some is sometimes perceived as a boring task, a long drawn out religious duty, where one has to say the right words, and be in the right place. Wrong. It is not. Prayer is simply talking to God. Prayer can be both audible and silent. It is letting God know how you feel about various situations, problems, joys, etc. It can be said spontaneously from the heart, or it can be read as penned by yourself or by someone else who had been able to articulate what you want to say.

There are many kinds of prayers. Some are prayers of thankfulness. Others are petitions for special graces or favours, still others are prayers of confession, where one offers prayers of repentance to God. One such prayer is that of the uniformed professional, King David as is so beautifully recorded in Psalm 51:1-13. David wrote:

> **1** Be merciful to me, O God, because of your constant love. Because of your great mercy wipe away my sins! **2** Wash away all my evil and make me clean from my sin! **3** I recognize my faults; I am always conscious of my sins. **4** I have sinned against you—only against you—and done what you consider evil. So you are right in judging me; you are justified in condemning me. **5** I have been evil from the day I was born; from the time I was conceived, I have been sinful. **6** Sincerity and truth are what you require; fill my mind with your wisdom. **7** Remove my sin, and I will be clean; wash me, and I will be whiter than snow. **8** Let me hear the sounds of

joy and gladness; and though you have crushed me and broken me, I will be happy once again. **9** Close your eyes to my sins and wipe out all my evil. **10** Create a pure heart in me, O God, and put a new and loyal spirit in me. **11** Do not banish me from your presence; do not take your holy spirit away from me. **12** Give me again the joy that comes from your salvation, and make me willing to obey you. **13** Then I will teach sinners your commands, and they will turn back to you. (**GNT**)

Enjoy the ride and don't forget to pray. Pray often, not only when the road of life is bumpy but also when it is smooth. To begin this book of prayers, please allow me to say a little prayer for both of us.

Dear Lord:

As an 'emergency services' chaplain, I want to first of all thank you for the privilege of serving those who serve as uniformed professionals. Please help me and my fellow chaplains and other community clergy who serve alongside. Please give us much guidance and discernment as we endeavour to care our professionals in uniform.

I pray especially for these front line service members whose work puts them in harms way. I pray for their protection. I pray that you will grant them wisdom and discernment for the day to day decisions that need to be made. I pray your blessing on their families. I pray for those who have experienced setbacks because of accidents, sickness, stress, etc. Grant them renewed strength and courage.

May the prayers and reflective questions included here in this book be a source of encouragement and enablement for each. These things I humbly ask in your Holy Name, Amen.

We will now move on to the series of eighteen different prayers as outlined in the Table of Contents.

Love And Romance

Dear Lord: My heart is pounding
It's one of those days
My sweetheart is around,
My head, I'll raise

I think he's/she's the one
It seems to be true,
I'm so much in love
Hardly know what to do

But with my job as You know
I need to be sure
It takes someone special
To fit the decor

As a unformed professional,
There's lots of stress
I want to do this right,
I want to give my best

So I wonder Dear Lord
Is he/she really for me?
In the midst of life's storms
Will we both be happy?

That he'll/she'll be there the day
That I walk down the aisle
But the days after too
For a long, long while

Will he/she be the one
With whom I'll grow old?
Will our love last forever,
Or will our passion grow cold?

Lord it's a very big step
That I want to make
I just need Your advice
Before the step I take

I know how I feel and
How my family feels too
What's important right now
Is how it's felt by You!

O Lord You know
What is best for me
And what the future holds
For my spouse to be

And I want the best
And I'm sure You do too
I want to be sure
Before I say "I do"

O Lord I need guidance
And direction today,
So I'll know for sure,
Exactly what to say

For marriage is serious
This I'll surely know
For the Good Book,
Undoubtedly tells me so

Life can be difficult enough
Without the added grief,
A spouse approved by You
Will be of much relief

The original plan for marriage
Is written in Your book
One man, one woman
No need for a second look

When Adam dozed off to sleep
You took from him a rib bone
You made Eve, his darling wife,
So he didn't have to be alone

The rib bone is near the heart,
Is where a spouse should be
An equal partner in every way
Seems very plain to see

The rib bone is beneath the arm
Designed to be protected
The other parts designed as well
We see to be connected

With this in mind, it seems so fine
That marriage is part of Your plan,
So for guidance and direction
Lord I need Your helping hand

Your Book speaks so clearly
About keeping of the vow
The time for discernment
Is really right now

While I feel really in love
I'll wait patiently until
You confirm in my heart
That it's Your perfect will

I need to please You Lord
In all that I do
In my life and in my work
Especially my marriage too

So here it is
I'm putting it all out
I really need Your guidance
So there isn't any doubt

So speak to me Dear Lord
Put Your peace within my heart
I need to have Your guidance
Right from the very start

Dr. Lorne K. Freake, Ph.D. (Padré)

When the day finally comes
For wedding bells to ring
I'll not be worried at all
Or be concerned of anything

So thank You Lord for my future spouse
I'm sure things will be ok
As we check in with You
Lead us O Spirit we pray

Amen

QUESTIONS WORTHY OF REFLECTION

1. What is Love?
2. Do you love your partner?
3. How often do you tell your partner that you love him/her?
4. How is your love generally expressed?
5. How do you demonstrate that love?
6. If you have any children, do you love your children?
7. Do they know that you love them? If so how?
8. How do you share your love with them?
9. Are love and respect the same?
10. If not, how are they different?
11. Love is spelled T-I-M-E
12. Do you agree? Why or why not?

My New Baby

Dear Lord: Our precious child has arrived
Planned or not we'll all survive
Seriously though we're really happy
With another person in our family

We have planned for this joyous event
Delivery day has come and went
Mother is fine and baby is great
Now more chores upon our plate

The night time feedings, the crying too
Sometimes I don't know what to do
It seems all new but it's been before
I just couldn't remember any more

But I remember now, I haven't forgot
Babies also need changing in their cot
It doesn't always smell like perfume
Sometimes I just want to leave the room

But it's my baby, I can really see
God the great gift You've given me
That precious soul is just a child
I'm busy now, I'll be for a while

Preschool stage seems easy to me
With daycare too since we're busy
But then again it costs a lot
For someone else to care for our tot

I wonder if it's worth being on the job
While baby goes off to daycare with a sob
Lord there must be a better way
So I can see my baby during the day

Shortly then it's off to school
Where my child has to be cool
The pressure today it's more than enough,
For our kids with all that stuff

So Lord, how am I doing?
Will I overcome?
Are You pleased with my progress?
Will it be a job well done?

Lord I know You've given me
A great instruction book
And in it often Lord,
I should somehow take a look

Lord I really want to do this right
So my baby will be safe and bright
The book is the B-I-B-L-E
Where it's all written, plain to see

Help Lord me to read it,
And then to put it into use
So my parenting skills then,
Will really get a boost

I know that it's all in there
As written from the past,
It all makes sense somehow,
I can count on it at last

Lord thank You for my new baby
I'll be the best parent I can be
I'll be patient, wise and loving
So my baby can clearly see

That I'm a parent who loves
And really cares a lot
Especially for my baby,
My little tiny tot! Amen

QUESTIONS WORTHY OF REFLECTION

1. My baby, child, or children is (are) a gift from God. Agree or disagree?
2. How do you think your baby/child/children see the world?
3. How do they see **you** in their world?
4. One of the best resources of wisdom and thought about raising children is found in the Book of Proverbs in the Bible. There are actually thirty-one chapters in all in there, one per day for the whole month. In reading through it, write down some of the key words about children that you come across.

I've Been Promoted

Dear God: The exams are written, the results are in
I've passed the test, happy I'll grin
There are now possibilities to a world unknown
Wherever it is Lord will soon be shown

So what does a promotion mean for me?
Higher rank? Extras bucks? More authority?
I'll take it all, it's easy to grasp,
But along with all that, comes additional tasks

So now more bucks, means more taxes too
It's always tax time when the year is through
With a higher rank, more authority You say?
It couldn't be better any other way!

More authority means more responsibility to do,
Promotions are great, but I'll work harder too
"To whom much is given, much is required",
So harder I'll work and the more I'll be tired

Unless of course I discover the clue,
Ask You Lord to help me know what to do
It's important I know as the Good Book says
'Trust in You Lord, You'll direct my ways'

You'll give me wisdom as I need it
Smart folks are those who heed it!
So now I am promoted, it's good to thank You God,
You'll be with me today as I onward trod

I'll make some mistakes as we all know,
As I trust in You, You'll make me grow
I'll try to conform to Your exact desire
And You'll be with me . . . until I retire

So now I'm promoted
Some will tip their hat,
Yet have to work much harder
With more of 'this and that'

God You've been gracious,
It's so easy to see
I'll keep my feet on the ground,
My eyes to the sky and I'll make it, safely!

Amen

QUESTIONS FOR REFLECTION

1. What is the first thing that comes to mind when you think or hear the word "promotion"?
2. Do you think that all promotions are good?
3. Are there any negative effects on being promoted? If so, can you name them?
4. Do you think that all promotions are fair?
5. Are there folks who are promoted, who don't really deserve it?
6. Are there those who really do deserve it and are not promoted? If so, what is your reaction?

Moving Again

Lord do I really need it?
Is it worth anything at all?
Shouldn't I just leave it?
Is it worth another haul?

I've already moved it many times,
But never quite used it well,
Will I ever need it, ever?
It's so really hard to tell!

The space is often limited
The moving truck is small,
There's so much stuff to pack,
My back is against the wall

The kids say 'dad, don't chuck it',
The spouse is not impressed,
I've hardly seen it used at all,
Like most of all the rest

It seems each time we throw it out,
Next week we need it bad,
It is as if we should have kept
All of what we've had!

Most times we can never find,
These things 'in case we need'
So off to the store we go to buy,
Again and again indeed

Life is a little crazy,
When it come to moving time,
We minimize the spending,
In our efforts to save a dime

So Lord, help me to decide
What needs to be left behind,
What the Red Cross needs are,
For others to happily find

Most of what I have,
Is only stuff anyway,
Lead me to do as You will
Whatever it is, will be ok

When I wonder of the value
Of everything I own,
I know there's never a reason,
To complain, fret or moan

We are really just too spoiled,
We should live with less You know,
So when it comes time for moving,
We can simply pack and go

Amen

QUESTIONS WORTHY OF REFLECTION

1.   Why would you want to move?
2.   Where might you want to move?
3.   What are possible advantages of moving?
4.   What are possible disadvantages of moving?
5.   How does your family feel about moving?
6.   Do they generally adjust well after they move? Why or why not?
7.   Are the things you purchased more valuable to you at the point of purchase than they are to you later on?
8.   Is moving **on**, always the same as moving **up**? (Discuss)

Wisdom

Dear God: Did I make a mistake?
Or did I well discern?
Need I giv'em a break?
Will they ever learn?

It really tough at times,
When I'm out there on the beat
Have to always watch my back
When I'm out there on the street

Folks don't always want to help,
Like they used to in the past
Can't trust anyone anymore,
Some will give you a blast

Wonder why it's like that now
When I work so really hard?
Pressures come from all around
Must be always on my guard

Still not all folks are bad out there
Some just need a break
They need some understanding
Because life is so hard to take

Their kids are somewhat perturbed,
They have troubles in the schools
Life is a little ungluing
Some folks break the rules

Some kids don't know who their daddy is
Or to where they'll be moving next
They seem so vulnerable you know
It's enough to make you vex

Jobs are cut both on left and right
The bills are pilling high
The parents are all stressed out you know,
It's enough to make me cry

In the high risers and the projects
It's concentrated grief
I wonder if it'll ever end Lord
Or when they'll get relief

Everyone comes from somewhere
They all have a story to tell,
Some have had such terrible lives
It has been a living hell

So as a uniformed professional
Who is out there on the beat
I am asking Lord for wisdom
As I am working on the street

Lord I really need discernment
So I can right decide
Who's out there who needs my care
Who has no place to hide

Amen

QUESTIONS WORTHY OF REFLECTION

1. How do you define wisdom?
2. Can you think of some particular case when you really lacked wisdom?
   a) At work?
   b) At home?
3. Are there situations that come to mind where people were hurt or offended by your lack of wisdom?
4. If so, have you ever thought about apologizing to them because of this?
5. When at work, what is your source of wisdom?
6. When at home, what is your source of wisdom?
7. Who is your model of a wise person? Why?

Teenager Blues

Stop that again,
You're driving me crazy
You're out of control
You're somewhat lazy

Look at your room,
It's all a mess
Hang up your clothes,
Clean up your desk

Lord I've said it over
And over again
But it really seems
Useless to complain

The kids today
Don't give a care
About their chores
Or what they wear

Lord I'm trying real hard,
I've done my best
You will have to help me
With all of the rest

The kids out there
Are out of control
It doesn't exactly look like
The days of old

Where have we gone
So terribly wrong?
And why is it so hard
To try and continue on?

Why can't we ever
Really get along?
Lord, I can hardly wait
For them to move on!

And go on they will,
To another town
And leave me alone
To finally rebound!

Somehow I'll survive,
I know all of this
But for right now
It isn't real bliss

I wonder Dear Lord
Did I treat my parents this way?
Surely God I didn't
Dear God dear I say?

History seems
To repeat itself,
Lord how bad my dear parents
Must have felt

For a person in uniform
It's really hard,
I'm supposed to be
Always on my guard

Lord my dear family
Needs to be civilized
I'll admit Lord,
Yes, I've idolized

I seem to forget that
Kids will be kids
Professional's kids too,
Can lose their lids

My kids are the exact,
As the kids next door,
Somehow though, Lord,
Society expects so much more

It's the same for the child
Of a lawyer or teacher,
Or that of a judge, doctor,
Banker or preacher

Our kids too I know,
Really need a break
Sometimes the pressures
Are too hard to take

Kids will be kids
We're are told all the time,
Yet there are exceptions,
For those kids of mine

We are the professionals,
People in uniform,
Our kids are supposed
To be saints when they are born

O come on folks
Give us a break
Our kids are like others
Who like ice cream and cake

They are normal as anyone
In every sense of the word,
We will not let them be labelled,
A geek or a nerd

Even though we are officers,
Firefighters and the like,
Our kids are still kids
Who all like to bike

And all things like
Other kids like to do,
Music and sports
And yes partying too

Someday, they'll grow up
And will all leave home
Leaving us as parents
Tired and alone

That's what it's all about
And very simple to see,
As kids are a part,
Of our blessed family

So yes, Lord at times
We've all had it rough
But through it all,
We have become tough

It's official of course,
And we'll all survive,
It's the continual goal
For which we strive

So with Your help Lord,
We should try to relax
Try as we might,
And stick to the facts

After all Dear Lord,
It isn't all that bad
With all of Your help
One day we'll be glad

So thank You Lord,
For my teen(s)
Help me Lord
Not to be mean

When they're all grown up,
I want to be their hero,
So help me dear God,
Not to be a zero!

Amen

QUESTIONS WORTHY OF REFLECTION

1. Write down ten words that typically describe a teenager?
2. How does your teenager fair in that general description?
3. Teenager is a child in transition from childhood to adulthood, do you agree?
4. As a parent, how do you think you could facilitate the process?
5. What are some of the values you wish your child/teenager had?
6. Have you personally modeled those values for them?
7. If you could be a teenager all over again, how would you do things differently?

$\mathcal{D}ebt$

Dear Lord: I'm somewhat over bent
Because I definitely over spent
I've been hurting to the bones
Trying to keep up with the Jones

It's all that advertising
That's got me appetizing
It's the latest tech and gizmo
That has taken all my dough

Plus now everything cost so much,
I really don't need all that stuff
So help me get it straighten out
I'm sure You can, there is no doubt

I'll cut up the credit cards first of all
Before I'm driven up the wall
And I'll go back to the simple ways,
Like it was in the good old days

Back then I watched every dime
And my needs were met all the time
If I didn't have the cash to buy
I didn't buy it on the fly

So now I'll have to take a look
And keep a budget in a book
And rid myself of things I don't need
I'll be the example, so help me lead

I know that I need to set the rules
While at first it won't be cool
My family will follow this I know
There is no choice, it will be so

I'll shop more wisely first of all
And keep my budget on the ball
I'll ask You Lord to be my guide
So I'll be on the winning side

I'll even be kinder to the poor
I'll give donations at the door
I'll be less selfish that's for sure
Helping others, I was created for

I'll be more thankful for what You've done
Life for me will be more fun
Being in debt will be of the past
Prosperity and blessing will come at last

Now that I have it all figured out
I am relieved there is no doubt
I'll have what I need to pay the bills,
Without the debt that always kills

There will be more money for the little things
For simple pleasures which the happiness brings
And less events will now go wrong
Because of the budget that I am on

I might even give more to the local church
For its causes are of much worth
It supports the poor at home and abroad
It definitely does the work of God

So thank You Lord again and again
Thanks is offered to Your Holy Name
I've learned Your lessons You wanted to teach,
I'm glad they were still within my reach

I'll do things different so much better now
Because of Your grace You have taught me how
I'll slow down a little more and seek Your advice
Your care and concern for me are really nice . . . ! Amen

QUESTIONS WORTHY OF REFLECTION

1. How much debt is too much debt?
2. What are the factors that determine whether or not you make a purchase?
3. When you buy something you really can't afford to, how do you justify the purchase?
4. What happens when you buy something that you simply didn't need?
5. How is the value of something determined by you?
6. Reflect on this statement: Value is determined not by what you pay for it, but rather the maximum amount that you can get for it if you had to sell it?
7. What percentage of your purchasing is directly affected by advertising? By need? By want? By peer pressure? By family desire?

Professional Conflict

Dear God: It's bound to happen
Now and then,
By misunderstandings,
From way back when

We perceive something
That isn't true,
It happens more
Than a time or two

There really
Isn't any bad intent
Something wasn't given
It was rather lent

But O what a
Surprise to find
My good will gesture
Has been left behind

I know that this
Happens at all levels
As people are perceived
As being devils

Oh but that is
Extreme you say,
None the less
It happens anyway

But why do we react
With such ugliness?
Truth is that is happens
To most of us

Lord we seem
To get all upset
It happens to all,
We shouldn't fret

But Lord, why
Are we like this?
Why at times
Do we lift our fists?

Why don't we
Just tip our hat?
There is a better way
To deal with that

There is a better way
To be understood
And all of us can,
If dare we would

So let's do it right
And avoid the shout
And give each other
The benefit of the doubt

It makes a whole
Lot more of sense,
Unless of course
We're really dense

Of course we're not
We're the pros
But like it or not
Everyone knows

Dr. Lorne K. Freake, Ph.D. (Padré)

That we should
Work more together
In sunshine and rain
In all kinds of weather. Amen

QUESTIONS WORTHY OF REFLECTION

1.   Why can't everyone get along?
2.   What is necessary for team work?

Personal Conflict

Dear Lord: next time someone
Walks on my shoes
Help me with my temper
Not to lose

Enable me Lord
To be full of grace,
By putting myself
In that person's place

It's often only
A false perception
Yet somehow we fail
To make the connection

After all Lord,
We're on the same team
But our reactions are
Too often in the extreme

So please help me Lord
To do much better
I'm so wrapped up,
In myself, is what's the matter

A little less of me maybe,
And a little more of You
Is exactly what I
Should attempt to do

Whether in the office Lord
Or out on the street
Or in some dark alley,
Out on the beat

We are really more alike
That we are different
Harmony shared here,
Should be our intent

So help me dear Lord
To walk side by side
I invite You as well
To be our guide

For each one of us,
Is a person unique
May other's well being,
Be our goal to seek

Somehow Dear Lord,
I am less worried now,
I've had time to reflect,
And I can see how

That it is so
Easy to judge
When we all fail
And hold a grudge

But when we give,
The other a break
The conflict then seems
So easy to take

When we're ready to walk
In the other's shoes,
We're less preoccupied
With our P's and Q's

We can relax a little more
And then try to be nice
There's more to this story,
Is real good advice

So help us Lord to
Work more together
And to understand more
Will even be better

Amen

QUESTIONS WORTHY OF REFLECTION

1. How long ago were you in some sort of personal conflict?
2. Do you know why or how it happened?
3. Do you know if it was resolved?
4. What are some of the dynamics that create personal conflicts?
5. What do you usually try to do in order to avoid such dynamics?
6. What are some of the coping skills to have in avoiding conflicts?
7. What lessons have you learned along the way so far?

Trauma

Dear Lord: The body parts were scattered
All across the road,
The broken glass was shattered
Underneath the load

While it happened long ago
Now years in the past,
Can't seem to forget it
As memories last and last

It was really trauma
And in the first degree,
Untold tragedy for sure,
For my innocent eyes to see

It scared me then
And it scares me now
Can hardly get over it,
I do not know how

It's a mark so deeply
Engraved in my brain
For which now at present
I can still complain

Lord I need Your help
In a desperate way
I need this gone forever
Or at least kept at bay

I will survive this
I surely know
But the nightmares
Will have to go

But O I'm a pro,
In a uniform
I've been taught over again,
That this is the norm

It's so very true
At the end of the day
The memories are here,
And they won't fade away

So Lord I'm asking
What did I get?
Post trauma stress disorder,
I'm guessing it's safe to bet

At present You see,
I do not really know
But sooner or later
The signs will likely show

I guess Lord
I must be in grief
If only Lord,
I could get some relief

It has stolen my joy
And my energy too,
I can't seem to know
Exactly what to do

I'm thankful Dear Lord
What You wrote in Your Book,
For my grief and my sorrow
There on the cross, You took

I'm going to put in practice
What Your Book tells me to do,
Which is basically to trust
And put my confidence in You

Because You care for me,
So the Good Book says
And You will do it well
In so many different ways

So today, I'm saying goodbye
Indeed to all my sorrow,
I'll change my way of thinking,
Starting now and not tomorrow

I no longer need to be
Now burned out by stress
With Your grace and help,
I'll get through the rest

It's been a long time coming Lord,
But now I'm almost there
I know now for sure that,
You have answered my prayer

So by faith and by Your grace,
I'll say a prayer today
To thank You Lord for all Your help
Providing for me a way

I feel much better now
And will get on with the task
You have taught how simple it is,
Just to come to You and ask

We know that You want
Indeed to bless all of us
You're are not at all alarmed
By any of this fuss

Amen

QUESTIONS WORTHY OF REFLECTION

1. Stress for you means what?
2. What are some of the symptoms when you are under stress?
3. What do you do for leisure, pastime or hobbies?
4. How do you deal with things that you can not change?
5. Ever talked to God about was stresses you?
6. Interested in reading some verses in the Bible that talk about stress? If so, take a look at these references: Matthew 6:25-34, I Peter 5:7.

Justice Denied

Dear Lord: I've seen it before and I'll see it again
I'm talking about justice denied
The court case was solid, we did our work
Yet apparently someone has lied

It's kind of strange when we do it all right
And apparently there's no doubt at all
But in the courts, the system aborts
And justice is pushed to the wall

They cling to some clause in the Charter of Rights
To have a case for their take
A smart alic lawyer with way too much power
Pleads a great case for his/her sake

It is not always about truth,
It's more about winning we see,
As justice gets denied and emotions subside,
It's not at all the way it should be

So our streets are not as safe as they should be
Nor will they be for a while,
Technicalities get people off the hook
Some charges are not worthy to file

Lord in spite of the system's faults
And all of our real time hurts,
Help us to remain faithful to it
As one day it might be of worth

Lord guide us to change the things we can
And to do it our very best
And to accept what we can not change
And then leave to You the rest

So Lord, let Your kingdom come,
Where justice and righteousness reign
Help us improve on the status quo
And it will reduce our pain

Amen

QUESTIONS WORTHY OF REFLECTION

1. What is justice?
2. How is justice and mercy different?
3. Does God care about justice issues?
4. How do you define truth?
5. Is the justice system better today than it was several years ago? Why or why not?
6. How would you improve on it if it was up to you?

Justice Served

Dear God: I can't always say it is this way
But today I see the results
Often times it's so easy to see
That the system has its faults

It's difficult when we do our job
And then expect others to follow
But when in court we come up short
And then we're left there in a hollow

But the results today were very good
And the thugs are off the street
Investigators did an excellent job
And the Crown turned up the heat

The judge could see it was in vain
To let the thugs go free
The system is far from perfect Lord
But today was, as it should be

But help us Lord to keep the faith
In You and the system too
We'll work at it with all our might
It's the least that we can do

So thank You God for the reward
For those who have done their job
The community is safer now
And we've done the work of God

Amen

QUESTIONS WORTHY OF REFLECTION

1. What does justice mean to you? To victims?
2. What are some justice issues that are very important to you?
3. What are some justice issues that are less important to you?
4. Where do you think God fits in, in justice matters?

Officer Down

Dear Lord: I've always feared it would happen
But never thought it would be
On a shift with my own comrade
But now . . . a reality

Lord it hurts so much to see
That it happened this way
I never saw it coming
Especially on this day

We've lost a member
Who we really respected
We worked well together Lord
We were well connected

What if I have done things otherwise
I'll always ask myself
The results might as well be different
If choices were differently felt

But Lord there's a hurting family
Who'll react like there is no tomorrow
How will they deal with such a loss?
Please bless them in their sorrow

Not only them but the department too
How will we get it together?
We need Your help dear Lord, we really do
And with it we'll all be better

With an officer down
We're asking why
Why did this officer,
Our friend have to die?

For a uniformed professional
This is a concern
What are the lessons
Here for us to learn?

More ready . . . the next time?
So much more ready prepared
In the meantime Dear Lord,
It hurts a lot, feels really weird

To be without our comrade
Who was so dear to us,
Not sure we can move on,
But move on . . . Lord we must

Help us all to make sense
Of what has happened here,
Please help us, Dear God,
And keep us in Your care

Amen

QUESTIONS WORTHY OF REFLECTION

1. What are the concerns that you fear most happening on your shift?
2. Have you ever thought about how you would react to a family of a comrade killed in the line of duty?
3. How would you like for your comrades to be of service to your family if you were to die?
4. What is your coping mechanism when you are faced with such reality on your job?
5. Where do you think pastoral care fits in?
6. Do you know the name of your chaplain?
7. Do you know his or her telephone number?

Grief—Death Of A Parent

Dear God: Seems like only yesterday
My teenage life was all hurray
And growing up was fun to do
My parents' guidance got me through

It almost seems as just last week
After high school, a career to seek
My parents expressed it was all ok
A promising career they seemed to say

So to higher studies I did go
And in greater knowledge I did grow
It seemed like time would last forever
My parents' death . . . a thought of never!

Life became busy with marriage plans
Followed shortly with wedding bands
The career began with promotions too
The time was spent before I knew

My folks became older and feeble they were
I failed to see the limits of their future
But now the reality of life has set in
It's good to reflect now and then

Their funeral services were well organized
And folks came from afar, I have realized
It's all over now but I need to say
I miss my parents who have passed away

While I can somewhat hide in my uniform,
I'm a hurting soul who needs to be warmed
By a kind word or thought or even a prayer
From someone out there who dares to care

Lord help me today to carry on
Beginning tomorrow at early dawn
You'll help carry me to the end,
Thanks for Your help Lord, I now say Amen.

QUESTIONS WORTHY OF REFLECTION

1. Is there something you wish you had said to your parents?

2. Is there something you wish you had **not** said to your parents?

3. You can not change the past, but you can change the way you see the past, true or false?

4. Have you shared your grief with a significant person?

5. Do you need someone to talk to?

6. Do you know the name and telephone number of your chaplain?

7. Interested in reading Bible verses that deal with the subject of grief? If so, look at the following: Isaiah 53:4-6, Matthew 5:4, I Peter 5:7.

The Passing Of A Child

Lord: it can't be true
It can't possibly be,
Why did it happen
To someone like me?

Not that I wish Lord
For it to be elsewhere,
But it seems so painful,
Almost too much to bear

I had hoped and prayed
For such different results
But that didn't happen,
Was it at all my fault?

It now seems so easy
To sit back and blame,
Myself, if not others,
Dare I mention a name?

"What if", I wonder and fret
And stay up all night?
If I were a better person,
Things might be alright

I'm hurting Dear Lord
And I'm hurting really bad,
This child was my child,
I'm so very, very sad

At first I could not believe
It just seemed so unreal,
Reality is settling in,
It's an awful way to feel

I'm really angry Lord,
I'm wound up very tight,
Can't seem to release the pain,
My grief hasn't taken flight

I never got to say good-bye
Some words were never said
When I think about it now,
Thoughts race within my head

But time now has passed,
And I can not go back,
I live with only memories Lord
Of which there is no lack

I know I will survive it
By grace in all due time
But now it's always there
Continually on my mind

I know Lord You understand,
Our troubles are a few,
Pain is now between us
And grief is nothing new

So when I talk about my loss
You know just what I mean
I can let it all hang out,
What is, has already been

You've told us in the Bible
In which we get our belief
That You came, in Your Name
To help bear all our grief

It's so clearly written
In Your Holy Book
All our sins and grieves to bear,
So help me take a look

In Matthew 5, You remind us too
How blessed are those who mourn,
For comfort will come, it surely will
To those whose hearts are torn

So please help me Dear God
As I try to continue on,
I'll soon feel much better,
When my grief is finally gone

Amen

QUESTIONS WORTHY OF REFLECTION

1. Can there ever be any comfort after the death of a child?
2. Where is God when it hurts?
3. Parents never get over the death of a child, they only get through it. Do you agree or not? (Discuss)

Divorce

Lord: I didn't plan it to be this way,
But it has happened what can I say?
It all seems so unreal right now
I need Your guidance as I humbly bow

I wonder Lord what You think of it all
All matters to You both great and small
We all need direction to continue on,
So help us Lord with a sense to belong

It doesn't feel right and maybe it shouldn't
Changes were needed but maybe we wouldn't
In any case now it seems like it's over,
not exactly seen in a four leaf clover

Much water now is under the bridge
And photos are no longer stuck on the fridge
Many words were said that we need to forget,
Honestly Lord . . . I'm not over it yet

We all know Lord there are really two sides,
Both mine and my ex's and none of it lies
It's not about blame for what has been done
neither about shame of what has become

Forgetting is one thing but then to forgive
Is the only way that we can actually live
If I forgive her/him, then You can forgive me,
It now seems so easy, for me to see

Lord I just want to hear Your heart beat
To know that You're with me though my faith is weak
I still need to hear Your still small voice
So in my brokenness, I can still rejoice

Lord I can go on forever thinking, "what if . . ."
But I choose rather to live with "what is . . ."
Forgive me O God and help me to forgive myself too
And to be forgiven by those I've hurt, even You

Amen

QUESTIONS WORTHY OF REFLECTION

1. Are there any issues concerning divorce that you have never addressed?

2. Do you ever feel that you need to be forgiven by someone?

3. Have you ever asked them for forgiveness?

4. Do you feel that someone needs to be forgiven by you?

5. Have you ever thought of ways in which you could facilitate this forgiveness process?

6. Are there any particular *thoughts* that you are thinking right now? If so, what are they?

7. Are there any *emotions* that you are feeling right now? If so, what are they?

8. Do you want to discuss this issue with the chaplain? Why not give him or her a call?

Sickness

Holy One:
We need to talk
About recent news
From the Doc

Been tired much lately,
Was wondering why
I now know for sure
And I want to cry

Life wasn't supposed
To be this way
I was doing so fine,
Now I've gotta pray

Do You hear me Lord?
Are You listening now?
I'm drowning in tears,
On my knees I bow

I haven't been keen
On this religious stuff
I've been so busy
And if it wasn't enough

Night shifts and courses
It comes and goes
I've been lately so tired,
And why no one knows

But You know dear Lord,
Please help me please
I'm shaking and trembling,
I fall on my knees

I'll read Your Good Book,
I'll be better for sure,
Just give me a chance,
So I can serve some more

I'll even go to church,
More than twice per year,
I'll curse a lot less,
I'll drink less beer

I'll behave more wisely,
I'll be a better spouse
I'll even help my partner,
Do more chores in the house

Oh God, can't You see
I'm in a desperate way
I really need Your help
Please help me today

I'm told in Your Book,
You've paid all out
For my sins and my sickness
Grace is what it's about

So here I am Lord,
I give You my heart
Forgive me O God,
Give me another start

I'm thanking You in advance
For Your wonderful grace
I'm much obliged
That You died in my place

It was a very cruel cross
And You bore it so well
You paid the full price
To save me from hell

So now Lord You see
I'm not doing so well
You see I have troubles
It's so easy to tell

I can only ask and believe
You'll work it all out
Whatever You decide
Will be best is no doubt

In the meantime,
I'll wait while I humbly ask
For grace and strength
To keep up with the task

I'm committing now
To Your guidance and care
That Your grace is sufficient
Is no burden to bear

Bless my dear family
As I'm sure You can do
The end of the story
Is all up to You

My prayers are the same
So I'll soon say Amen
We should talk more often
Instead of just now and then

A good Lord You are
And a good Book You wrote
Been so busy lately
Nearly missed the boat!

So now trials have come
And sickness my way
Would You help me to focus
On yet another day?

I'll say goodnight for now
I won't keep You up late
I'll just trust in Your grace
Instead of my fate

So goodnight again Lord
We'll talk some more soon
While I dose off to sleep
I'll hum You a tune

I can now clearly see
Your purpose and plan
It's a hard lesson to learn
But now I understand

You really care for me
That's all that really counts
Your love, grace and mercy
Comes in large amounts

So good night again Lord
I feel much better now
I'll sleep like a baby
You have well taught me how

Amen

QUESTIONS WORTHY OF REFLECTION

1. Why do you think there is sickness in the world? What lessons in life are learned through sickness?

2. How does our value system change when we are confronted by sickness? Are there things that you want to say to someone, since having to deal with your own sickness?

3. If you have received prognosis from your doctor, have you thought about getting a second opinion?

4. Have you called your pastoral care agent to talk about these issues?

5. Do you know of any verses in the Bible that would give you encouragement concerning your time of sickness? Here are some: I Timothy 6:6-8, I Peter 5:7, James 5: 14-16.

Retirement

Dear Lord: This what I've waited for
To finally walk out the door
To finally leave for one last time
With never nothing on my mind

Lord I've been there and have done that
Now it's time to hang up my hat
I'll put in my last run
I won't be back, won't that be fun?

My spirit is really lifted high
I finally get to say goodbye
I won't even say "see you soon"
"Goodbye for ever" will be my tune

Lord I wonder if I've made my mark
During the day and after dark
Will the world be a better place?
Because I was here and filled this space?

Will the time I've spent have any effect?
Did I make a difference? Did I connect?
Was anyone changed because of me?
Did I do my very best, maybe?

I wonder Lord if I'll miss this place
Never again will it see my face
I'm leaving now that's for sure
And I won't be back anymore

Now that I'm gone, will anyone care?
Will they say, "thank you?" Will they dare?
I really doubt it and I don't care why
Because I finally get to say "goodbye"

Now Lord what is my next step?
Surely You are not through with me yet!
I still have a contribution to make
Where will it be, my next step to take?

Lord, "Who is in need of my expertise?"
Who will benefit from talents such as these?
Lord, I'll go where You please
So guide me now while I'm on my knees

Is it to some foreign field?
To help poor people, a crop to yield?
Is it to help build an orphan's house?
Or to far away fire that needs to be put out?

Maybe I should go far away somewhere
Instead of wasting my talents so dear
Maybe on a mission's trip overseas
Send me Lord wherever You please

I'm sure there still something I can do
I want to be available to work for You.
It's not just enough to finish my task
I want to be doing what You'll ask

I've course I'm retired there is no doubt
But meaningful volunteerism is what I'm about
So where should I go? What should I do?
I really want to be guided by You

Lord I thank You for my generous pension
It will help me live freely without any tension
I will be able to pay all my bills
I just want to discover Your will.

I'll stay here in North America
If that is Your plan
If not, I'll go
To a far away land

Oh Lord: I'm retired
And I've got it made
I have no mortgage
My house is paid!

So are all of
My other things
My dog who barks
And my parrot who sings

Life has changed
And my values too
I now want to
talk more often to You

I want Your opinion Lord
On where I should go
Because right now,
I can go with the flow

Please lead me Lord,
By Your voice within
And please forgive me
Of all my sin

I'll be more wiser
This time around
Whether I'm up or
Whether I'm down

What matters now
Is what matters most
I'm now retired and
I have left my post

So today is a new day
I'm out again I'm on my way
No more uniform for me to don
Retirement, thank God, Bring it on! Amen

QUESTIONS WORTHY OF REFLECTION

1. Is there any particular task that you have never completed while you were working that could be revisited now that you are retired? List the talents/gifts/expertises that you have developed which might be of value in the non-profit sector of your community. How about overseas?

2. Have you thought about volunteering activities in your faith community?

3. Now that you have the time, have you thought about catching up with people with whom you've lost contact?

Conclusion

As a Padré, it is my hope that each one of you have found something special in this book. Hopefully, you have not experienced all the difficult times written about here, but to those of you who have encountered such, I hope that you were able to find some inspiration and answers to your prayers. I would like to conclude by offering a final prayer. Unlike the others in this poetic prayer book, (18 in total), I didn't write this one. It comes to us from St. Francis of Assise, 1182-1226.

I believe where you are, as a uniformed professional; whether you are a member of the Armed Forces, Police Officer, Peace Officer, Firefighter, Security, Customs or Correctional Officer, etc., you are called to fill this particular role as an instrument of God's peace. Hence, as a chaplain who ministers to you and to your colleagues, I invite you to join with me and St. Francis in this special prayer:

Lord, make me an instrument of your peace,
Where there is hatred, let me sow love;
where there is injury, pardon;
where there is doubt, faith;

where there is despair, hope;
where there is darkness, light;
where there is sadness, joy;

*O Divine Master, grant that I may not so much seek to be
consoled as to console;
to be understood as to understand;
to be loved as to love.*

*For it is in giving that we receive;
it is in pardoning that we are pardoned;
and it is in dying that we are born to eternal life.*

Amen

Epilogue

Blessed are the merciful for they will receive mercy. Blessed are the pure in heart, for they will see God. Blessed are the peacemakers for they shall be called children of God.

Matthew 5:7-9 (**NRSV**)

Articles And Collections

Holy Bible, Good News Translation (GNT), Canadian Bible Society (Catholic Edition), Ottawa, Ontario, Canadian Conference of Catholic Bishops, copyright @ 1994, 1742 pages.

Holy Bible, New Revised Standard Version (NRSV), Division of Christian Education of the National Council of Churches of Christ of the USA. New York, New York. copyright @ 1989, 1376 pages.

Web Pages/Links

www.adopt-a-cop.org

www.americanpolicechaplaincyassociation.org

www.chaplainfederation.com

www.christianchaplain.com

www.cndpolicechaplains.org

www.copcare.ca

www.firechaplaincy.org

www.flfop89.org

www.icpc4cops.org

www.ipfca.org

www.ministrymatters.ca

www.nca-hq.org

www.peaceofficersministries.org

www.policechaplains.org.uk

www.thecenturionlawenforcementministry.org

About The Author

Dr. Lorne K. Freake (pronounced Free-ak) is an ordained minister with the Convention of Atlantic Baptist Churches. He has served as a pastor and a Bible college teacher. Presently he volunteers as a Chaplain (Padré) for the RCMP—District 10, "J" Division and the Grand Falls Fire Department, in North West New Brunswick, Canada. He also serves as a member of the local Critical Incident Stress Management (CISM) Team.

He is the Director of Ministry Advancement (DMA) for the Canadian Bible Society for Atlantic Canada.

Dr. Freake and his wife Peggy (a high school guidance counselor) are the proud parents of four 'young adult' children.

Notes

Notes

Notes

Notes

Notes